THE BUM JOKE BOOK

compiled by Hugh Jarse
illustrations by R. Sole

WARNING: This is the only serious page in this book!

ELITE Words & Image
P O Box 24, Sherborne, Dorset, DT9 3SN

British Library Cataloguing in Publication Data
Jarse, Hugh
The Bum Joke Book.
I. Title II. Sole, R.
8.28.9140208

Printed in Great Britain by Cotswold Printing Company Ltd
Origination and Imagesetting by Cotswold Printing Company Ltd
Typesetting by Stable Design & Print

ISBN 0-9516677-1-8

ACKNOWLEDGEMENTS

I should like to express my thanks to my friends, Rod and Moira, for their interest and misguided encouragement!

And, to Bob for his insatiable and inspirational sense of humour.

A special thank you to my family and friends (far and wide) who have, by now, dispossessed me!!

Hugh Jarse

Other books in this series:

Pile in the Road by G G Dunnit
Bubbles in the Bath by Ivor Windybottom
Yellow River by I P Daley

and on a more academic note ... Fart Calculus by Dr A Puffadder

Published by: Uranus Publishing, Bottomly Street, Windem.

Typeset in Bumface

Printed by Mooning Printing Services
(no job too big or too small)

Page Layout and Design by Craphardt & Pugh Imagesetting

Illustrations by R Sole ©
Compiled by Hugh Jarse ©

Printed on Recycled Loo Paper - our strength is our softness.

This is it ...

shh ... don't tell a soul ...

BUM'S THE WORD !

A RHYME FOR GUFFY

A wonderful thing is a fart,
It lives in the Valley of Bum,
And when it is time to depart
It gives you a warning hum!

PISSPRONUNCIATION

"Pissoles and mash, please."
"Pissoles?"
"Yes, pissoles - there, that's what it says on the menu."
"Er, that's an R, sir."
"All right then, arseholes and mash, please."

A HOSTESS WITH THE MOSTEST

After a night out the young man asks her if he can come back to her place. She agrees but says, "All right, but you'll have to be very quiet so as not to wake my parents."

Later, at her place, he asks if he can go to the toilet. The girl replies, "Yes, but you can't go upstairs, you'll have to use the sink in the kitchen."

Shortly, his head appears around the kitchen door and he asks, "Have you got any paper?"

Fritz Gerhardt Produkts
Conradstrasse, Munchen, Germany

Customer Services,
Great Western Food Company,
Houston, Texas, USA.

Dear Sirs

Der last drie schipments off der rice ve get from you vas mitt der mice schidt mixt. Der rice vas guttenoff but der mice durds schpoils der trade. Ve did not see der schidt in der schamples vot you sent.

It tages too much time to pick out der schidt from der rice. Ve order kleen rice, und you schipped schidt mit der rice.

Ve like you to schip us der rice in von sak, und der schidt in annuder sak, und den ve can miks to soot our customers. Plis write if ve schud schip back der schidt und keep der rice, or keep der schidt und keep der rice, or keep der schidt und schip back der rice, or schip back der holdt schitten vorks.

Ve vant to do ride in dies matters, but do not like dis mice schidt buziness.

Mit much respekt,

Fritz Gerhardt

ODD JOBS

"Gad, sir? Did you fart?"
"Of course, I did my man: do you think I smell like this all the time?"

A MINOR SLIP UP

A small little man with his umbrella and briefcase walks into a bar and immediately slips on some excrement on the floor.

The little man picks himself up, goes to the bar and buys himself a half a lager and sits at a table by himself.

A little later a strapping great brickie enters and slips on the excrement. "I just did that," quips the little man - the brickie breaks his nose.

A MODICUM OF DECORUM

A rich and respected society lady held an afternoon tea party for her influential
friends and ate more cucumber sandwiches than she ought. During one of
those deadly silences that happen, even at the liveliest of parties, a colossal
breaking of wind came from the direction of the hostess.

Never one to be easily embarrassed the lady turned to her butler and said,
"Forsythe, stop that immediately."
"Certainly Madam," said Forsythe,
"Which way did it go?"

HEAR, HEAR

Wife: "You know dear, Rover's hearing isn't as good as it used to be."
Husband: "Nonsense. Come here Rover, now sit."
Wife: "There, I told you so."
Husband: "All right dear, I'll clean it up."

ODD JOBS

Why do farts smell?
For the benefit of the deaf.

ASS NO QUESTIONS

Father O'Leary was a priest in a very poor parish and was asking for suggestions on how to raise money for his church. He was told that racehorse owners always seemed to have plenty of money. So Father O'Leary decided to go to the next horse auction, but not knowing much about horses he made a very poor buy; as the horse turned out to be a donkey!

However, looking on the bright side, he thought he might as well enter the donkey in a race. The donkey came third. Unfortunately, this came to the notice of the local newspaper editor who was no friend of Father O'Leary's, and to prove this the next morning the headlines read "FATHER O'LEARY'S ASS SHOWS". The Bishop read the paper and was most displeased. In the next race the donkey came in first and the headline read, "FATHER O'LEARY'S ASS OUT IN FRONT". The Bishop was now up in arms and figured something had to be done. Father O'Leary had entered the donkey for a third race and this time it came in second. Now the headlines read, "FATHER O'LEARY'S ASS BACK IN PLACE".
The Bishop thought this too much, so he forbade the priest to enter the donkey in any more races - this inspired the headline "BISHOP SCRATCHES FATHER O'LEARY'S ASS".

Finally the Bishop ordered Father O'Leary to get rid of the donkey. He was unable to sell it and so gave it to Sister Charity as a pet. But, the next day read, "NUNS OWN BEST ASS IN TOWN".

When the Bishop read this he ordered Sister Charity to get rid of the animal at once. She sold it for twenty pounds. Next day the headlines read, "SISTER CHARITY PEDDLES HER ASS FOR TWENTY POUNDS". They buried the Bishop three days later.

"I SUPPOSE" STORY

Overheard conversation involving a farmer from Stoke Sub Hamdon -

"I went to the doctors as I've 'ad this problem with constipation. The doctor gave me some suppositories, tellin' me to put 'em in me back passage when I got home and they'd sort me out in no time. Well, bein' as we 'aven't got a back passage, I put 'em in the porch.

Mind you, fat lot o' good they've done too. I might just as well've put 'em up me ass!"

Why are turds tapered?

So that your bum doesn't close

with a BANG!

A JIMMY RIDDLE

A man was lost in fog and snow on the Pennines. At last he saw a light so, going up to a cottage, he knocked on the door. A little boy answered.

"Is your father in, son?" asked the man.

"No," said the boy, "if he was in I wouldn't be."

"Oh," said the man. "Is your mother in?"

"No," said the boy, "but if she was in neither I nor my father would be."

"Have you any brothers or sisters?" asked the man in desperation.

"Yes, sir," said the lad, "one sister but she isn't in either. Mind you, if she was in neither father, mother nor I would be."

"This *is* a funny house," said the man, who was quite frustrated by now.

"Not really," said the boy, "this is the toilet."

HAD TO BEE DONE

Once upon a time an American on a freeway had to do some No.2's. Having stopped, he got out to relieve himself. As he returned to his car he noticed a cop car stopping behind his.

Panic stricken he rushed back to his pile and covered it with his hat. At that moment a rugged policeman asked why he had stopped contrary to the Traffic Regulations. The man replied that he had a huge bee in his car, had stopped, and chased and trapped it under his hat.

The heroic cop decided to end the days of the poor little bee and promptly attacked the hat with his truncheon. The man asked the condition of the poor little bee. The vicious police officer lifted the hat and inspected.

"Is it dead?" asked the man.
"Dunno, but I've sure given it a heck of a fright."

What's the difference between a baby and a seagull?

One flits across the shore ...

What's the difference between a bad marksman and a constipated owl?

One shoots but can't hit ...

3 ... 2 ... 1 ... BLAST OFF!

One lunch time a farmer noticed his favourite cat stagger through the door with its coat dull and bedraggled, ears drooping and with a most miserable expression on its face. The farmer was very worried so he rang the local vet who was a little deaf. After reciting a detailed list of the cat's symptoms to the vet a gallon of castor oil was prescribed.
"A gallon?" queried the farmer in surprise.
"That's right, one gallon," said the vet and rang off.

Later that day the vet rang to see how the patient was.
"How's that cow, now?"
"Cow, what cow?"
"The cow I prescribed a gallon of castor oil for."
"That was no cow, that was my CAT!"
"Oh, NO," said the vet. "What's it doing now?"
"It's out in the orchard with twelve other cats."
"And what are they all doing?"
"Well," said the farmer, "as far as I can see, there are four digging, four filling in and four scouting ahead for fresh ground."

THERE'S NO BUSINESS LIKE MONKEY BUSINESS

A man goes to his Doctor to complain that he is pregnant. The Doctor informs him that it's just not possible and tells him that he is only suffering from constipation. However, the man insists that he is pregnant. The Doctor decides to give him some pills to relieve his problem and gives him instructions on how to use them. When he gets home he is to put a cork up his bum, take the pills and then go to sleep. When he wakes up he is to go the bathroom, remove the cork and retire to a safe distance from the toilet. The man is still convinced that he is pregnant but decides to follow his instructions.

Later, as he sleeps, a recently escaped monkey climbs past his window, seeing the cork he becomes curious. On climbing inside he watches and waits then decides to remove it! The blast flattens him against the opposite wall. The noise wakes the man who immediately dashes over to the dazed animal. Wiping the poo from the monkey's face he says, "I don't care how ugly you are you're mine and I love you."

COMES OUT SMELLING OF ROSES

A man goes to the doctor complaining of a pain in the rectum. The doctor tells him to slip his trousers off and bend over. The doctor probes around and after a moment or so he pulls out a daffodil. He probes around some more and brings out another daffodil, and another, and another, until in the end he is standing there with half a dozen daffodils in his hand.

"Look here," he says to the patient.
"A half a dozen fresh-cut daffodils - have you any idea how they got there?"
"No," he says, "is there a card with them?"

Doctor, Doctor, why is it that every time I go to the toilet it comes out as chips?

Try lifting your string vest a bit higher.

Doctor, Doctor, what is that you're writing with?

It's an anal thermometer - some bum's got my pen.

ATHLETE'S FOOT, TENNIS ELBOW, CRICKETER'S BUM ...

A young man, obviously in agony, waddled into his doctor's surgery.
"What's wrong with you?" enquired the doctor.
"I've got a cricket ball lodged in my rectum."
"How's that?" pursued the doctor.
"Now don't you start."

IT'S ALIMENTARY, MY DEAR WATSON

A man who fell into the canal was pulled out by a passer-by who started to give him artificial respiration. Water was pouring out of his mouth but he still wasn't breathing; so the rescuer turned to the crowd that had gathered and asked:

"Does anyone know anything about artificial respiration?"

A little man in a suit said, "No, but I do know something about hydrostatics." The rescuer looked at him curiously but carried on. Water streamed from the man's mouth and he still wasn't breathing. The rescuer asked the crowd again only to get the same reply from the little man. The crowd yelled, "Shut up!"

He carried on, but to no avail, so he said to the little man:
"Okay, what do you know about hydrostatics?"

"Only that if you don't get his bottom out of the water you'll pump the canal dry."

ODD JOBS

"Mummy, mummy, has the Au Pair got a detachable bottom?"
"No darling. What on earth made you think that?"
"I just heard Daddy say that he'd like to screw the ass off her."

ODD JOBS

What is brown and steams on a piano seat?
Beethoven's Last Movement.

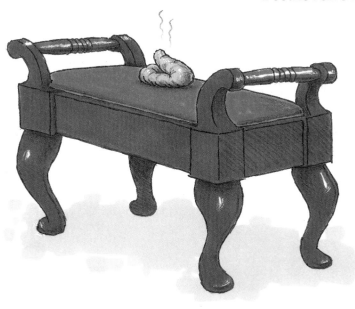

A HISTORY LESSON

Nelson was sailing The Channel one day, when the Look-out sighted three French ships,
"Three Froggies off the port bow, Sir," he called down.

"Thank you, Mr Look-out," replied Nelson, then turning to his cabin boy asked him to
fetch him his red coat, as they were about to engage the enemy. At this, Hardy questioned
Nelson's motives, as wearing red would make him stand out and be an easy target for any
French sniper. "If I'm wounded and my men can see the blood on my coat they will lose
heart for the battle and we will lose. But, Mr Hardy, if I wear my red coat and I am
wounded, then the blood will not show and my men will continue to fight."
Hardy marvelled at the bravery of the Admiral and had even more respect for him. The
battle was joined and the French ships soon put to flight.

Soon the Look-out called down again to Nelson,
"Twenty Froggy ships on the starboard side, Sir."

Nelson looked up and called out to the Look-out.
"Thank you Mr Look-out," then turning to his cabin boy said,
"Go to my cabin and fetch me my brown corduroy trousers."

KNICKERBOCKER GLORY

The boy stood on the burning deck,
the flame about him flickers.
He shouted, "I don't care, what the heck,
For I have asbestos knickers!"

A NAVAL RHYME

'Twas on the good ship Venus...

The first mate's name was Chopper,
By Gad, he had a whopper!
Twice round the deck,
Once round his neck,
And then, up his arse for a stopper.

BEAN AND GONE

There was a man who adored baked beans but they had a very unfortunate side effect on him. As he was soon to be married he resolved to give them up. With admirable willpower he managed this, although the withdrawal symptoms ruined his honeymoon. He refused to eat baked beans ever again to stop himself returning to his nauseating habit.

For five years he denied himself even a single bean. Then, on his fifth wedding anniversary he was going to fetch his wife from town when his car broke down. He started to walk back to a garage he'd passed when he smelt a wonderful smell - baked beans. The smell was coming from a cafe just opposite and it was totally irresistible. He thought, just one plateful could do no harm and by the time he got to his wife his problems would have disappeared in a puff of wind!! Later, his car repaired, he went to pick up his wife.

On the way back home his wife said that he must go into the house with his eyes closed, go straight to the bedroom, change and wait until she came to fetch him. This he did. On her return she blindfolded him, lead him downstairs and sat him at the dining table and then ... the phone rang. She went to answer it. While she was away he felt a great fart welling up inside him, then he let go quite involuntarily, he listened, it was all right his wife was still talking. Feeling much relieved, he farted again, worse than before and the smell was terrible. He picked up a napkin and wafted it furiously until the smell had dissipated. He listened again, his wife was still talking, the performance was repeated with a much louder and much more revolting eruption; still his wife was talking.
Eventually she returned and removed his blindfold with a flourish to reveal 12 dinner guests sat at the table!

A LANGUAGE OF HIS OWN!

A well known Colonel had a servant called Wibble, who did everything his master
told him. One day the Colonel said,
"Run me a bath, Wibble," so Wibble ran a bath.

Once in the bath the Colonel ask for a radio; then some tea, some hot towels and
then his pipe.
Then Wibble hears, "Water bottle, Wibble."

Wibble rushes to fetch a water bottle. Handing it to his master he says,
"Your water bottle, Sir."

"But I didn't asked for a water bottle, Wibble," says the Colonel.
"Farting in the bath again, Sir?"

ODD JOBS

What's the definition of a laxative?

An extrashit missile.

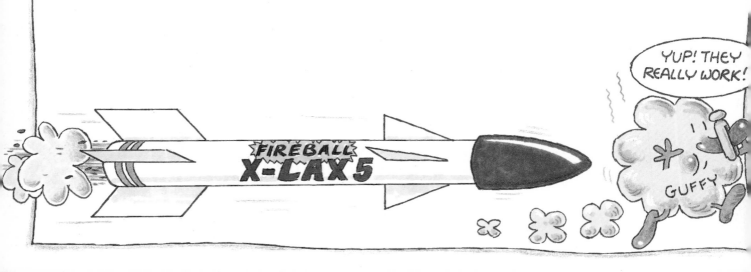

A RHYME FROM DOWN-UNDER

There was an old man from Australia
Who painted his bum like a dahlia
A penny a smell was all very well
But tuppence a lick was a failure

A TIMELY END?

A boy and girl were walking home late one night when the boy began to feel rather passionate. So they decided to stop for a bit on the way.

They were passing the local graveyard so went in and became very amorous!

When the girl got home she complained of a back pain. She stripped and asked her mum if she could see anything wrong.

"Well," said her mum, "there's nothing wrong with your back, but your bum died in 1881."

A WEE RHYME

Good luck to the man who eats brown bread,
He farts like roaring thunder,
He shits gert rolls like telegraph poles,
Until the earth goes under.

HUGH JARSE AND R SOLE
would be pleased to hear from any reader
who has enjoyed reading
THE BUM JOKE BOOK
and ask that if you have any bum jokes
that you would like to contribute,
THE BUM JOKE BOOK
FART TOO!
will shortly be in the making.

This will, of course, be followed by
THE BUM JOKE BOOK
DER TURD PART!

(Acknowledgements will be made)

THE END

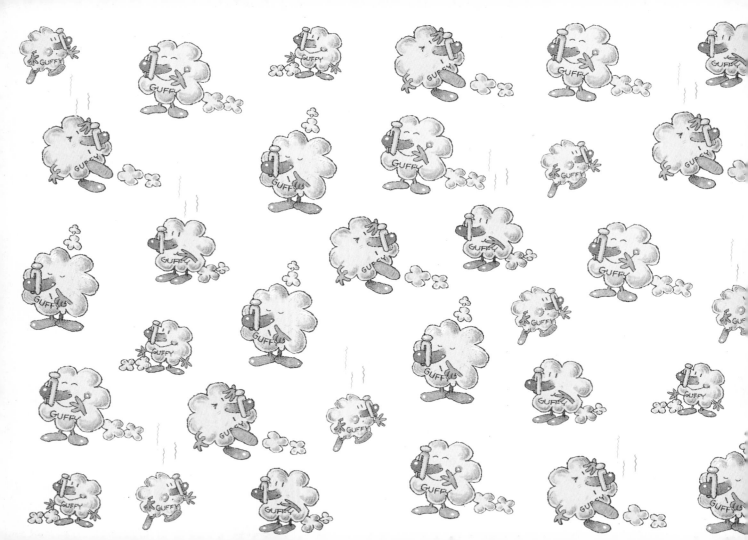